GET
WELL

RONALD SEARLE

Zoodiac

PANTHEON BOOKS · NEW YORK

Copyright © 1977 by Ronald Searle

All rights reserved under International and Pan-American Copyright Conventions. Published in the United States by Pantheon Books, a division of Random House, Inc., New York. Originally published in Great Britain as *Searle's Zoodiac* by Dobson Books Ltd., London.

Library of Congress Cataloging in Publication Data

Searle, Ronald. 1920–
Zoodiac.

1. Astrology—Caricatures and cartoons.
2. English wit and humor, Pictorial.   I. Title.
NC1479.S39A4   1978   741.5′942   78-50030
ISBN 0-394-50062-8

Manufactured in the United States of America

FIRST AMERICAN EDITION

ARIES	♈	22 March to 20 April
TAURUS	♉	21 April to 21 May
GEMINI	♊	22 May to 22 June
CANCER	♋	23 June to 23 July
LEO	♌	24 July to 23 August
VIRGO	♍	24 August to 23 September
LIBRA	♎	24 September to 23 October
SCORPIO	♏	24 October to 22 November
SAGITTARIUS	♐	23 November to 22 December
CAPRICORN	♑	23 December to 19 January
AQUARIUS	♒	20 January to 19 February
PISCES	♓	20 February to 21 March

For my own
personal Virgo

♍

ARIES

TAURUS

GEMINI

CANCER

LEO

VIRGO

SAGITTARIUS

CAPRICORN

AQUARIUS

PISCES